Illustrated Would You Rather? by Dr. Shh
Silly Kids and Family Scenarios, Book 1

ISBN: 9781794316065

Published by Dr. Shh
Amsterdam, Netherlands

TABLE OF CONTENTS

PART 1 - CRAZY SCENARIOS

DISCLAIMER: SOME OF THE SCENARIOS MENTIONED AND DEPICTED IN THIS BOOK CAN BE POTENTIALLY DANGEROUS. DON'T TRY THIS AT HOME.

WOULD YOU RATHER

go on vacation and have a shark living in your swimming pool

or

go on vacation and have a T-Rex living at the beach?

WOULD YOU RATHER

have all teddy bears in the world turn into actual bears

or

have all computer mice in the world turn into real mice?

WOULD YOU RATHER

have the largest eyes in the world like a giant squid

or

be unable to blink your eyes like a fish?

WOULD YOU RATHER

have to wear a bowl of spaghetti tipped over
your head every time you watch a cartoon

or

have to wear raspberries on your fingers every
time you go out?

WOULD YOU RATHER

throw stuffed animals at each other with your friends in the toy shop

or

play sock snowballs in the movie theater with your classmates?

WOULD YOU RATHER

get a birthday cake prepared by a five-year-old baker

or

get a haircut from a five-year-old hairdresser?

WOULD YOU RATHER

have to crawl in a very long and narrow underground tunnel to get to school

or

have to go to school in a shopping cart with pedals instead of a bicycle?

WOULD YOU RATHER

have a magical giant rabbit which you can ride like a horse

or

have a magical giant flying dragon on which you can ride?

WOULD YOU RATHER

have a swim ring or a lifesaver on while you play volleyball

or

wear an M&M's costume while you play basketball?

WOULD YOU RATHER

drink a mixed Coke, Sprite, and Fanta beverage

or

eat a pepperoni, banana, and strawberry pizza?

WOULD YOU RATHER

play "The Floor is Lava" game in the room
where there is actually lava on the floor

or

play hide and seek in a cave full of monsters?

WOULD YOU RATHER

raid your piggy bank to buy a huge set of back scratchers

or

stay 150 nights in different hotels for the purpose of collecting "Do Not Disturb" signs?

WOULD YOU RATHER

have to spend a day cracking and shelling nuts to feed a hundred hungry squirrels

or

have to spend a day digging carrots to feed a hundred hungry rabbits?

WOULD YOU RATHER

invent a magic super salad making you four times as strong as you are

or

invent a magic super smoothie that makes you a four times faster runner?

WOULD YOU RATHER

discover an intelligent pig that can knit

or

discover an intelligent horse that can play chess?

WOULD YOU RATHER

compose a very stupid song titled *"I love sausages in my ice cream"* and get an award for it

or

become well-known for creating an odd superhero named Broccoliman who saves the world by eating tons of broccoli?

WOULD YOU RATHER

have to eat your breakfast tomorrow in the kitchen full of harmless snakes

or

have to eat your dinner tomorrow at a dark attic full of harmless bats?

WOULD YOU RATHER

have to wear a monkey costume for a whole day at school

or

have to act like a monkey in the grocery store until a random person tells you: *"Stop acting like a monkey"?*

WOULD YOU RATHER

go to the *"Harry Potter and the Cursed Child"* Broadway show in the costume of Lord Voldemort

or

attend Disney's *"Aladdin"* musical in the costume of the genie?

WOULD YOU RATHER

have the unique ability to swim faster than a shark

or

have the unique skill to run faster than an ostrich?

WOULD YOU RATHER

wear disposable rubber gloves instead of insulated gloves on a very cold winter day

or

wear a laundry basket on your head instead of a cap on a hot summer day?

WOULD YOU RATHER

construct a giant LEGO room and live in it

or

construct a giant LEGO car and drive it?

WOULD YOU RATHER

manually write the page numbers in ten huge books

or

manually delete 1,000 contacts from your phone?

WOULD YOU RATHER

watch all cartoons and videos in slow motion
at 1/4th speed

or

watch all cartoons and videos at 2x speed?

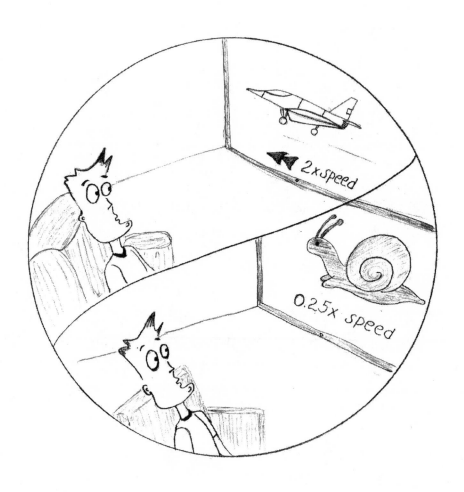

WOULD YOU RATHER

learn how to speak in the voice of any person

or

become the world's first person who can sing like a bird and understand their language?

WOULD YOU RATHER

tell *"Sixth sick sheik's sixth sheep's sick"* tongue twister fifty times every morning before you can have breakfast

or

tell *"How much wood would a woodchuck chuck if a woodchuck could chuck wood"* tongue twister fifty times every night before you can fall asleep?

WOULD YOU RATHER

spend one summer month under house arrest in your room

or

spend one summer month in a village without electricity?

WOULD YOU RATHER

have a real magical flying carpet that can
actually transport you anywhere

or

have a real magic 8 ball that can actually
predict the future?

WOULD YOU RATHER

use banana leaves instead of plates for your meals as people often do in many tropical countries

or

always have to eat with your bare hands?

WOULD YOU RATHER

go to a strange birthday party where all guests play chess instead of celebrating

or

go to a strange wedding where the bride and groom and all the guests play soccer at the restaurant where the reception is being held?

WOULD YOU RATHER

take mimicry lessons at school and learn how to mimic the sounds of motor vehicles, home electronics, and animals

or

take drawing lessons at school and learn how to draw super realistic cartoon heroes?

WOULD YOU RATHER

play bowling with a watermelon

or

play tennis with a balloon?

WOULD YOU RATHER

always have to wear very heavy shoes that would make it extremely hard to walk

or

always have to wear very slippery shoes that would make you feel like you walk on ice?

WOULD YOU RATHER

fly on an airplane with 300 people who cough without covering their mouths

or

fly on an airplane with 300 people who chaotically play musical instruments and sing songs as loudly as possible?

WOULD YOU RATHER

participate in the Italian Battle of the Oranges where people throw oranges at each other like snowballs

or

take part in *La Tomatina*, the Spanish tomato throwing festival?

WOULD YOU RATHER

eat a lemon burger and drink an onion cola for lunch

or

eat a baked bean sandwich and drink a pineapple garlic smoothie for dinner?

WOULD YOU RATHER

step in dog poop every time you have a bad thought about any person

or

own a big dog that poops ten times a day in random places, and that you would have to clean after it?

WOULD YOU RATHER

own the world's largest collection of different banana stickers

or

have more different water bottle labels than anyone else in the world?

WOULD YOU RATHER

peel fifty oranges each time before you can use an iPhone for half an hour

or

peel and chop ten onions each time before you can use an iPad or a computer for half an hour?

WOULD YOU RATHER

own a talking parrot that tells crazy jokes and tickles kids

or

own a funny puppy that can ride a scooter and play the ukulele (guitar-like Hawaiian musical instrument)?

PART 2 - CRAZY QUESTIONS GAME

HOW TO PLAY CRAZY QUESTIONS GAME?

1. Gather a few friends, parents, grandparents, or bring this book to your class and ask your teacher if every student can play.

2. Get a pen and some paper for each player.

3. Each player should write down numbers from 1 to 80.

4. Start reading these believe or not crazy questions. Answer "Yes" or "No", writing down the answers for each of the 80 questions. As soon as you finish, add up the number of correct answers listed in PART 3 of this book.

5. Find out who answered best of all!

READY? LET'S START!

1.   Do you believe that in 2017 a young great white shark was washed up on Manly Beach in Australia and temporarily put into a public saltwater swimming pool by the rescuers?

2.   Do you believe that the largest tooth of T-Rex ever found is 24 inches (60 cm) long?

3.   Do you believe that one of the teddy bears' first creators wrote a letter to then U.S. President Theodore "Teddy" Roosevelt asking him for permission to name the bears after him?

4.   Do you believe that the original computer mouse, which was built in 1964 and offered for sale in 1968, was a rubber drum with a single button?

5.   Do you believe that some species of sharks can blink to protect their eyes when they feed, which is something that no other species of fish can do?

6.   Do you believe that the giant squid's eye can be as large as 26 inches (66 cm) in diameter, which is the size of a mountain bike wheel?

7.   Do you believe that some turtles, hamsters, bunnies, cats, and even dogs love to eat raspberries?

8.   Do you believe that some people eat spaghetti with lion's head meatballs?

9.   Do you believe that some people cut socks, put fiberfill inside and sew "snowballs" to play indoor "sock snowballs"?

10. Do you believe that in 2018 hockey fans in Pennsylvania set the world's Teddy bear toss record by throwing 14 thousand stuffed animals onto the ice?

11. Do you believe that in 2018, a five-year-old girl became a certified barber and started offering free haircuts to kids in Philadelphia?

12. Do you believe that a five-year-old baker started a successful business in Florida by baking cookies and selling them in church after the service?

13. Do you believe that a shopping cart with pedals actually exists and has an alternative name – a trolley-bike?

14. Do you believe that 600 tunnels have been constructed under highways and roads in the Netherlands to help increase the population of endangered animal species such as the European Badger by preventing them from being hit and killed by motor vehicles?

15. Do you believe that the Continental Giant, the largest breed of rabbit, weighs up to 80 lbs (36 kg)?

16. Do you believe that the biggest parrot, Hyacinth macaw, can grow as tall as 3.3 feet (1 meter) as measured from the top of its head to the tip of its tail?

17. Do you believe that Lady Gaga wore a red M&M's costume to the 2010 Video Music Awards on MTV?

18. Do you believe that the swim ring which is also known as a lifesaver was invented by Walt Disney in 1920?

19. Do you believe that PepsiCo produced a yogurt-flavored Pepsi for sale in Japan?

20. Do you believe that the most popular pizza served at Formaggio Pizzeria in Sweden is the banana curry pizza?

21. Do you believe that *"The Floor is Lava"* game was invented in the 1890's in France?

22. Do you believe that some people play hide and seek with their cats?

23. Do you believe that a man from North Carolina has a record-breaking collection of 405 back scratchers?

24. Do you believe that a man from Italy has a collection of 5,000 "Do Not Disturb" hotel signs, which he personally picked up from the hotels where he stayed?

25. Do you believe that hungry rabbits can eat peppers, grapes, and mint leaves?

26. Do you believe that a very hungry squirrel can sometimes eat an insect such as caterpillar?

27. Do you believe that *"Fast Train"* was the original name of *"Innocent"*, a well-known smoothie producer?

28. Do you believe that fiambre is a salad from Guatemala which often contains more than 100 ingredients?

29. Do you believe that recent research studies have concluded that pigs are often smarter than dogs?

30. Do you believe that horses can distinguish between frowning and smiling human faces?

31. Do you believe that among the 10 most popular computer games ever are *"Grand Theft Auto V"*, *"Minecraft"*, and *"World of Warcraft"*?

32. Do you believe that the popular song *"Itsy Bitsy Spider"* is about 300 years old?

33. Do you believe that some snakes can sting with their tails?

34. Do you believe that bats can eat over 1,000 insects in the span of an hour?

35. Do you believe that the howls of the howler monkey can be heard from a distance of up to 100 miles (160 km)?

36. Do you believe that before 2018 Halloween monkey costumes were searched on Pinterest 6.8 times more often than in 2017?

37. Do you believe that there are 337 costumes used in Disney's *"Aladdin"* musical?

38. Do you believe that the Palace Theatre in London has the strange tradition of leaving two seats bolted open for the theater ghosts to enjoy the shows?

39. Do you believe that the Olympic gold medalist in swimming, Michael Phelps, swam faster than a great white shark in 2017?

40. Do you believe that the ostrich holds the record land speed of any bird, up to about 43 mph (70 km/h)?

41. Do you believe that the Odd Future brand of clothing is selling a cap that looks like a laundry basket?

42. Do you believe that disposable rubber gloves were invented by George Washington in 1781?

43. Do you believe that giant LEGO bricks are used today to construct real furniture and the walls in rooms?

44. Do you believe that in 2018, using LEGO Technic elements, LEGO presented its first life-size drivable car, a Bugatti Chiron?

45. Do you believe that the first phone book ever created consisted of only two pages?

46. Do you believe that someone found a World War II hidden radio inside an old book?

47. Do you believe it was reported in 2016 that every year YouTube users watch 46,000 years worth of content?

48. Do you believe that the number of TV shows has doubled from 2009 to 2019?

49. Do you believe that birds living in less polluted environments sing more complicated songs than birds living in more polluted areas?

50. Do you believe that Elvis Presley and Enrico Caruso (one of the world's greatest tenors) were once told by the experts that they couldn't sing?

51. Do you believe that the *"She sells seashells by the seashore"* tongue twister refers to a real woman who was digging seashells at the beach and found dinosaur fossils?

52. Do you believe that *"How much wood would a woodchuck chuck"* tongue twister was written in 1972 by Michael Jackson as a song?

53. Do you believe that one in twenty people in the world live without electricity?

54. Do you believe that in 2012, Okan Kaya from Australia broke the world record by playing the videogame for 65 hours?

55. Do you believe that the magic 8 ball was originally developed to promote billiards?

56. Do you believe that the original version of *"Aladdin and the Magic Lamp"* didn't mention the magical flying carpet?

57. Do you believe that it's healthier to eat off of banana leaves rather than plates because of the natural anti-oxidants contained in banana leaves?

58. Do you believe that when people eat with their bare hands in North Africa, two water bowls are placed in front of them: one for washing their hands before the meal and another for rinsing their mouths?

59. Do you believe that there is a wedding tradition in China's Yugur culture for the groom to shoot his future bride with a bow and an arrow?

60. Do you believe that in 2018, an English couple postponed their wedding plans so they could watch the England national football team play in the quarter finals of the World Cup?

61. Do you believe that Bugs Bunny debuted in the 1940 Warner Brothers cartoon *"What's up, Rabbit?"*

62. Do you believe that barking owls from Australia have the stunning ability to accurately mimic the sounds of the other forest inhabitants and even the sound of a chainsaw?

63. Do you believe that when you play bowling and score three strikes in a row, experienced

bowlers would use the term "Eagle" for this achievement?

64. Do you believe that tennis balls were originally black?

65. Do you believe that hairspray can often help make shoes less slippery?

66. Do you believe that the heaviest shoes ever walked in weighed 250 lbs. (113 kg)?

67. Do you believe that according to a research study at Otago University in Wellington, New Zealand, one in four people cough without covering their mouths?

68. Do you believe that flying with a cello on an airplane sometimes requires passengers to buy a separate seat for the musical instrument and that musicians often purchase cello insurance that covers flight damage?

69. Do you believe that 30 tons of oranges are shipped to Ivrea from Sicily where the annual Battle of the Oranges takes place because oranges are not a typical fruit for that region of Italy?

70. Do you believe that *La Tomatina*, the annual tomato throwing festival held in Spain, is the world's second largest food fight, beaten only by the Italian Battle of the Oranges?

71. Do you believe that in 2005, Onion Coca-Cola was launched in New Zealand on a trial basis and that the experiment was discontinued later the same year?

72. Do you believe that scientists have recently discovered black garlic growing on the slopes of some volcanoes?

73. Do you believe that stepping in dog poop with your left foot in Greece means good luck?

74. Do you believe that in 2015, the Japanese city of Izumisano launched an app to report dog poop and to create an interactive online map of dog poop problem areas?

75. Do you believe that the tiny fruit stickers you often see on bananas, apples, and other fruits and veggies are edible?

76. Do you believe that in 2009, Lorenzo Pescini from Italy collected 3,650 different water bottle labels and broke the world record?

77. Do you believe that people compete in pushing oranges with their noses for a mile in the shortest time?

78. Do you believe that chopped onions absorb bacteria and become highly poisonous if you leave them overnight in the fridge?

79. Do you believe that there is an official GoPro channel video of an orangutan that professionally

plays the guitar-like Hawaiian musical instrument, the ukulele?

80. Do you believe that a species of parrot known as the nocturnal or night kakapo can weigh up to 9 lbs (4 kg), which is the average weight of a housecat?

PART 3 - CRAZY ANSWERS

PLEASE DON'T READ THE ANSWERS BELOW
UNTIL YOU FINISH ANSWERING THE QUESTIONS
IN PART 2 OF THIS BOOK.

1. YES, it's correct.

2. NO, the largest tooth of T-Rex ever found was 12 inches (30 cm) long.

3. YES, it's correct.

4. NO, the original computer mouse was a wooden box with a single button.

5. YES, it's correct.

6. NO, the giant squid's eye can be as large as 10 inches (25 cm) in diameter, which is approximately the size of a dinner plate.

7. YES, it's correct.

8. YES, it's correct. But it's only the name of the dish. People don't eat lion's heads.

9. YES, it's correct.

10. NO, they set a record by throwing 34 thousand stuffed animals on ice.

11. NO, that girl was seven years old when she became a certified barber.

12. NO, that baker was eight years old when she started her business.

13. YES, it's correct.

14. YES, it's correct.

15. NO, the Continental Giant weights up to 50 lbs (23 kg).

16. YES, it's correct.

17. NO, Lady Gaga wore the meat dress on that day.

18. NO, the swim ring was invented by the Vikings several centuries ago.

19. YES, it's correct.

20. YES, it's correct.

21. NO, *"The Floor is Lava"* game was invented in 1950's in the USA.

22. YES, it's correct.

23. NO, his collection consists of 675 back scratchers.

24. NO, his collection consists of 15,000 "Do Not Disturb" hotel signs.

25. YES, it's correct.

26. YES, it's correct.

27. NO, *"Innocent"* smoothie producing company was originally called *"Fast Tractor"*.

28. NO, fiambre is often cooked from more than 50 ingredients.

29. YES, it's correct.

30. YES, it's correct.

31. NO, *"Grand Theft Auto V"* is the 17th most popular computer game ever, *"Minecraft"* is on the 24th position, and *"World of Warcraft"* is on the 41st position.

32. NO, the popular song *"Itsy Bitsy Spider"* is about 100 years old.

33. NO, it's a myth.

34. YES, it's correct.

35. YES, it's correct.

36. NO, in 2018 Halloween cow costumes were searched on Pinterest 6.8 times more often than in 2017.

37. YES, it's correct.

38. YES, it's correct.

39. NO, during the "competition" against the shark, the Olympic champion swam no faster than 6 mph

(10 km/h), while the great white shark swam 25 mph (40 km/h).

40. YES, it's correct.

41. NO, among Odd Future hats there is no such thing as a cap looking like a laundry basket.

42. NO, rubber gloves were invented after World War II.

43. YES, it's correct.

44. YES, it's correct.

45. NO, the first phone book published in 1878 had only one page.

46. YES, it's correct.

47. YES, it's correct.

48. NO, the number of TV shows has doubled even faster – from 2009 to 2015.

49. YES, it's correct.

50. YES, it's correct.

51. YES, it's correct.

52. NO, *"How much wood would a woodchuck chuck"* was actually a song written in 1902 by Robert Hobart Davis for the musical *"The Runaways"*.

53. NO, actually one in seven people in the world live without electricity.

54. NO, in 2012, Okan Kaya from Australia played the videogame for 135 hours.

55. YES, it's correct.

56. YES, it's correct.

57. YES, it's correct.

58. NO, the first bowl is for washing hands before the meal and the second bowl is for washing hands after the meal.

59. YES, it's correct.

60. YES, it's correct.

61. NO, Bugs Bunny debuted in the 1940 Warner Brothers cartoon *"Wild Hare"*.

62. NO, lyrebirds from Australia can mimic the sounds of the other forest inhabitants and even the sound of a chainsaw.

63. NO, three bowling strikes in a row are called "Turkey".

64. NO, tennis balls were originally white.

65. YES, it's correct.

66. NO, the heaviest shoes walked in weighed 323 lbs (146.5 kg).

67. YES, it's correct.

68. YES, it's correct.

69. YES, it's correct.

70. NO, *La Tomatina* is the world's largest food fight.

71. NO, it was Coca-Cola Raspberry launched in New Zealand on a trial basis.

72. NO, black garlic is a white garlic expertly heat-aged over several months.

73. NO, it isn't. However, stepping in dog poop with your left foot in France really means good luck.

74. YES, it's correct.

75. YES, it's correct.

76. NO, Lorenzo Pescini from Italy collected 8,650 different water bottle labels breaking the world record.

77. YES, it's correct.

78. NO, it's an urban myth.

79. NO, the official GoPro video features the orangutan that makes random sounds using the ukulele.

80. YES, it's correct.

REFERENCES

1. "Shark moves in to Australian swimming pool". BBC News. September 12, 2017.

2. "Tyrannosaurus Rex: Facts About T. Rex, King of the Dinosaurs". Live Science. October 17, 2017.

3. "Teddy Bear". Encyclopedia.com.

4. "Tales In Tech History: The Computer Mouse". Silicon.co.uk. October 15, 2016.

5. "Why don't fish blink, and if they do, how do they?" Apologetics Press. Discovery Magazine. February 1, 2012.

6. "Largest Eye in the World, Giant Squid". Smithsonian Ocean Portal.

7. "28 Animals Eating Berries Look Like Horror Movie Monsters". Bored Panda.

8. "Spaghetti with Lion's Head Meatballs". Food Network.

9. "Have an Indoor Snowball Fight!" Jessica Fisher. Life as Mom.

10. "Hockey fans set Teddy Bear Toss record by throwing 34K stuffed animals on ice". News Channel 8. December 4, 2018.

11. "7-Year-Old Becomes Certified Barber So She Can Offer Free Haircuts To Kids in Her City". Good News Network. September 29, 2018.

12. "Tiny baker: 8-year-old pastry chef runs thriving baking business". Today.com. October 14, 2016.

13. "The Trolley-Bike Makes Going from Aisle to Aisle Easier". Michael Hines. Trend Hunter. November, 24, 2011.

14. "Engineering Facts". Science Kids.

15. "Continental Giant". Rabbit Pedia.

16. "Hyacinth macaw. Biggest parrot of all". Parrots Joy. March 18, 2017.

17. "See What Lady Gaga's Meat Dress Looks Like Now — 5 Years Later". MTV. August 28, 2015.

18. "Summer Object: The Swim Ring". Marielle Brie. July 1, 2018.

19. "The Wild World of Japanese Pepsi Flavors". Kotaku. October 30, 2014.

20. "7 strange pizza toppings from around the world". Wanderlust.co.uk.

21. "You Can Thank 1950s Suburban Architecture for 'The Floor Is Lava'". Shaunacy Ferro. Mental Floss. May 28, 2018.

22. "Playing Hide and Seek with Your Cat". Mavdl. That is for My Cat. May 10, 2018.

23. "Largest collection of back scratchers". Guinness World Records.

24. "How One Man Amassed a Collection of 15,000 Do Not Disturb Signs". Cailey Rizzo. Travel and Leisure. March 21, 2018.

25. "Safe fruit, vegetables, herbs and plants suitable for rabbits". Save a Fluff.

26. "What Do Squirrels Eat?". Sarah Ryrie. Love the Garden.

27. "15 Things Hardly Anyone Knows About Innocent Smoothies". Lara O'Reilly. Business Insider. December 3, 2014.

28. "10 salads from around the world". Ilana Strauss. From the Grapevine. May 8, 2015.

29. "IQ Tests Suggest Pigs Are Smart as Dogs, Chimps". Jen Viegas. Seeker. June 11, 2015.

30. "How Smart Is Your Horse?" Jennifer Forsberg Meyer. Horse&Rider. July 31, 2018.

31. "Top 100 Video Games of All Time". IGN.

32. "Itsy Bitsy Spider". All Nursery Rhymes.

33. "Snake Myths And Facts". Phil Purser. Reptiles Magazine.

34. "Are Bats Dangerous to Humans or Pets?" Janhvi Johorey. Animal Wised. January 22, 2017.

35. "Monkeys Do Act Like Humans. You Won't Believe This is Real!" Yes Vegetarian.

36. "The 18 most popular Halloween costumes you can expect to see everywhere this year". Madison Vanderberg. Insider. October 3, 2018.

37. "7 fascinating facts about Disney's Aladdin The Musical". Robyn Munson. Digital Spy. October 25, 2017.

38. "20 incredible facts about theatre that you won't believe are true". Ben Hewis. WhatsOnStage.com. January 4, 2019.

39. "Michael Phelps 'Raced' a 'Shark,' Kind Of. Not Really." Victor Mather. New York Times. July 24, 2017.

40. "Speed of Animals: Ostrich". Speedofanimals.com.

41. "Odd Future > Accessories: Hats". Odd Future.

42. "How the rubber glove changed our world: A history of social hygiene - and how Toilet Duck has made our lives better". Roger Lewis. The Daily Mail. February 25, 2016.

43. "Giant LEGO bricks snap together into life-size modular furniture". Lucy Wang. Inhabitat.com. August 31, 2015.

44. "First Ever Life-Size and Drivable Lego® Technic Bugatti Chiron is a Pioneering Piece of Engineering and Design". Bogdan Gherasim. Lego.com. August 30, 2018.

45. "Telephone – Invented By Alexander Graham Bell". Easy Science for Kids.

46. "The Best Things Found Between the Pages of Old Books". Sarah Laskow. Atlas Obscura. February 15, 2018.

47. "Google acquired YouTube 10 years ago today". Paul Sawers. Venture Beat. October 9, 2016.

48. "I have found a new way to watch TV, and it changes everything". Jeff Guo. The Washington Post. June 22, 2016.

49. "Our Musical Birdbrains: Why Do Birds (And Humans) Sing?" Nicole Dean. Brain World Magazine. March 29, 2018.

50. "Why You Hate Your Voice and How to Fix It". Audrey Hunt. Spinditty. November 18, 2018.

51. "The forgotten history behind the world's most famous tongue twister". Stefan Andrews. The Vintage News. May 18, 2017.

52. "The Obscure History Of Three Most Famous Tongue Twisters". Pro Caffenation. Nida Ali. November 6, 2017.

53. "One in Seven People Live Without Electricity". Ben Bunker. Clean Power Planet. December 21, 2018.

54. "Man breaks record for longest gaming session, clocks 135 hours". Olivia Solon. Wired. November 19, 2012.

55. "Where Did the Idea for the Magic 8 Ball Come From?" Cydney Grannan. Britannica.

56. "The History of the Magical Flying Carpets". Ancient Origins. June 11, 2016.

57. "Why Indians traditionally eat food on banana leaf instead of plates?" Guruprasad.

58. "The Rules For Eating With Your Hands In India, Africa And The Middle East". Alisha Prakash. Food Republic. November 19, 2012.

59. "Top ten weird and wonderful wedding traditions from around the world". Hello Magazine. January 14, 2014.

60. "Football-mad couple rearrange their own wedding so they can watch today's England match". Peter Craig. Grimsby Live. July 7, 2018.

61. "The Top 50 Cartoon Characters of All Time". Nancy Basile. ThoughtCo. November 26, 2018.

62. "Lyrebirds mimicking chainsaws: fact or lie?" The Conversation. February 3, 2014.

63. "Say What? 5 Weird Bowling Terms You Haven't Heard Before". Zone Bowling. January 29, 2014.

64. "9 Weird Facts about Tennis". Tennis Canada. April 27, 2015.

65. "How to Make Shoes Less Slippery". Wikihow.com.

66. "Heaviest shoes walked in". Guinness World Records.

67. "One in four people don't cover their mouths when they cough or sneeze". Claire Bates. Daily Mail. July 13, 2010.

68. "Can I Fly with a Cello?" Cello Central.

69. "The Battle of Oranges: an Italian Carnival tradition". Italian Good News. February 9, 2017.

70. "9 Alluring Facts About The La Tomatina Festival". Paulomi Dasgupta. Tomato Heart.

71. "Here's The List Of The Strangest Coca-Cola Flavours Launched Across The Globe". Republic World. July 10, 2018.

72. "What is Black Garlic?" The Garlic Farm. October 21, 2015.

73. "The strangest French superstitions – and how to avoid them". Morgane Croissant. Expatica. December 5, 2018.

74. "Japan: City launches app to report dog poo". BBC News. September 15, 2015.

75. "10 little known facts about fruit stickers". Aol. May 8, 2016.

76. "Largest collection of bottled water labels". Guinness World Records.

77. "A Record with a Peel". Ashrita.com. November 22, 2007.

78. "Are Cut, Raw Onions Poisonous?" Jenny McCoy. Cooking Light. March 28, 2018.

79. "GoPro: Orangutan Plays A Ukulele". GoPro, YouTube channel. December 9, 2013.

80. "14 Fun Facts About Parrots". Michelle Z. Donahue. Smithsonian magazine. January 5, 2016.

A WORD FROM THE AUTHOR

THANKS FOR READING MY BOOK! PLEASE, HELP ME TO GROW BY PROVIDING YOUR FEEDBACK.

IF YOU LIKED MY BOOK, SUPPORT ME BY LEAVING A SHORT REVIEW ON THE BOOK'S WEBPAGE.

ALSO, FOR A LIMITED TIME YOU CAN SUBSCRIBE TO MY MAILING LIST AND I'LL BE SENDING YOU MY FORTHCOMING HILARIOUS CHILDREN'S E-BOOKS FOR FREE! CONTACT ME drshhbooks@gmail.com

THE END

Made in the USA
San Bernardino, CA
31 March 2020